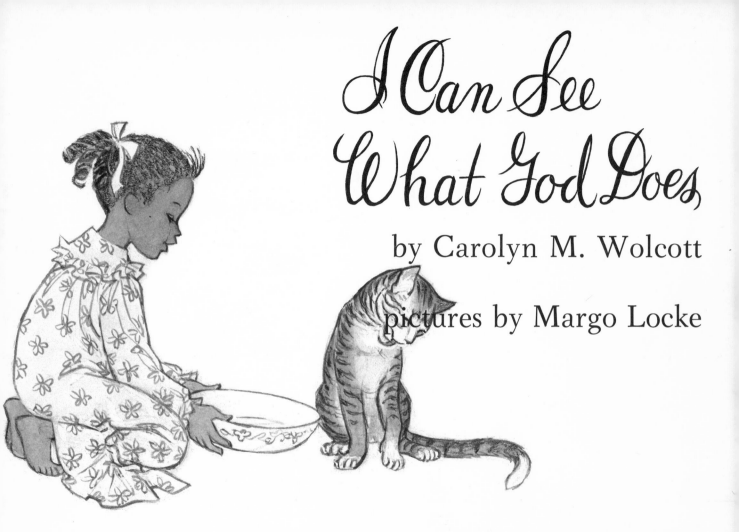

I Can See What God Does

by Carolyn M. Wolcott

pictures by Margo Locke

NASHVILLE   ABINGDON PRESS   NEW YORK

Copyright © 1969 by Abingdon Press   All rights reserved
Printed in the United States of America
Standard Book Number: 687-18424-X
Library of Congress Catalog Card Number: 69-16940

Swish, swish, swish
     blew the wind across the sky.
    Debbie watched the dust and papers
     swirling down the street.
    She saw the smoke from chimneys
     streaking out across the sky.
    She felt the wind tickle her nose
     and bite her ears.
She let it push her down the street
    and right in the front door
     of the building where she lived.

68994

"The wind is blowing," cried Mother, catching Debbie. "It is blowing hard."

"I know," said Debbie.
"It's so strong I had to go where it sent me,
and it sent me right home," laughed Debbie.
"It's noisy, too."

"Have you ever seen the wind?" Debbie asked Mother.
"I wish I could see the wind."

"No," answered Mother, "I have never seen the wind.
Nobody has ever seen the wind.
But we can see the things the wind does.
When we see the clothes blowing on the line
    and the drugstore sign flapping back and forth,
when we walk across the bridge
    and see the whitecaps on the river,
    we say, 'There's a strong wind
        blowing today.'

When we see the flag on the courthouse
flying out straight
and a hat rolling down the street
and white clouds hurrying along the sky,
we know the wind is blowing."

"Who made the wind?" asked Debbie.

"God planned the wind," said Mother,
"when he planned the world."

"I wish I could see God," said Debbie.

"You cannot see God with your eyes,"
                    said Mother,
        "just as you cannot see the wind.
    But you can see the things God does."

"Tell me how I can see what God does,"
                    said Debbie.
    "Tell me now
                while we wait for Daddy."

Mother and Debbie sat down by the window.
"Look out the window,
and tell me what you see," said Mother.

Debbie looked as far as her eyes could see.
"I see a river, wide and gray.
I see lights, winking and blinking.
I see a pigeon, shiny and white,
and a spot of oil in a puddle of water."

"Are they not beautiful?" asked Mother.
"Whenever we see anything that is beautiful
or anything that is true
or anything that is good,
we are seeing something
God has done.

God gave us colors to enjoy.
　　Red and yellow and green—
　　　　the colors of neon signs
　　　　　　and traffic lights.
　　Blue and gray and black—
　　　　the colors of sky and water
　　　　　　and smoke."

"And pigeons and sparrows and starlings," added Debbie.
　　"He made the pigeons white
　　　　and sometimes blue.
　　He gave the sparrows wings of gray
　　　　and the starlings feathers all black."

"That's right," said Mother.
　　"And he put many colors
　　　　in the spot of oil on the puddle of water."

"Listen," said Debbie. "What is that?"

"It is the sound of the wind as it howls
        between the buildings," said Mother.
    "Sounds, too, are part of the beauty
        God has put into the world.
    The coo of the pigeon outside the window.
    The sound of the rain
        splashing on the windowsill.
    The roar of the water
        as it pours from the fire hydrant.
    The singing of the teakettle."

"And Daddy when he comes in the door
        and says, 'Hi, everybody,'" laughed Debbie.
"Yes, and your own happy songs
        in the early morning," added Mother.

"Now tell me about things that are true," said Debbie.
  "What is true?"

"True," said Mother, "is anything that really is.
  Whenever people find out something that is true,
      they are finding out about God.
  When the astronaut discovers what is in space,
      and the scientist learns what is on the moon,
      and the doctor finds out what helps children grow,
      they are learning something true about God.
  They are learning how God works in his world."

"And when I am happy
        because I shared my toys with Bobby,
    am I learning something true about God?" asked Debbie.

"Yes, indeed," said Mother. "You are learning
        one of the rules for living happily
            in God's world."

"God is good," said Mother.
   "He gave us a good world,
   and we can see his goodness in many ways.
We can see it in the things
         he has put into the world
               for people to use—
      the rain that washes the air
            and cleans the streets
            and fills the rivers
            and gives us water;
      the electricity that lights our lamps
            and sends the elevator up and down
            and runs the subway
            and gives us heat."

"And people?" asked Debbie.
   "Is God's goodness in people?"

"Oh, yes," answered Mother.
   "When people are kind
      and love each other,
      when boys and girls are friendly
         and share with each other,
      then we can see God's goodness
         in people."

Debbie jumped up and clapped her hands.

"I'm glad," she said.

"I'm glad I can see what God does.

I'm glad I am part of God's good world."